SAVING OUR WORLD

ENDANGERED SPECIES

Mike Unwin

COPPER BEECH BOOKS
BROOKFIELD, CONNECTICUT

© Aladdin Books Ltd 2000
Designed and produced by
Aladdin Books Ltd
28 Percy Street
London W1P 0LD

First published in the United States in 2000 by
Copper Beech Books,
an imprint of
The Millbrook Press
2 Old New Milford Road
Brookfield, Connecticut 06804

Editor: Kathy Gemmell
Designer: Karen Shooter
Picture research: Brooks Krikler Research
Certain illustrations have appeared in earlier
books created by Aladdin Books.

Cataloging-in-Publication data is on file at the Library of Congress.
ISBN 0-7613-1211-0

Author Mike Unwin is a writer and editor based in London. He specializes in wildlife
and travel, and has written and edited a number of publications on these subjects.

Consultant David Burnie is a zoologist who has worked on a variety
of natural history titles for adults and children.

ABOUT THIS BOOK

This book is divided into chapters that guide the reader
through the topic. First, we examine what being an
endangered species means. We then look at the reasons why
specific creatures—and the places where they live—are in
danger of vanishing, and take a close look at the role that
humans play in this disappearing act. Finally, we discuss
different conservation measures, what is being done
to find out more about endangered species, and how
we can work together to protect them and the places
where they live. Throughout the book, stimulating **Talking
Points** raise greater awareness and provoke discussion about
the important environmental topics and issues covered in the book.
These are reinforced at the end of the book by a **Look Back and
Find** section, where questions test the reader's newfound knowledge
of the subject and encourage further thought and discussion.

CONTENTS

Species in Danger

Disappearing act

All over the world, many different species of animal and plant are in danger. Some are disappearing altogether. We don't know exactly how many species exist today, but we do know that the number is getting smaller all the time. People are the main cause of this sad disappearing act. We are using up more and more of the planet for our own needs. We kill animals for food, sport, or money, or just because we can't learn to live with them. We cut down forests, poison the oceans, and destroy precious land to build farms, factories, and cities. We are even causing the climate to change by polluting Earth's atmosphere.

There are only about a thousand giant pandas left in the wild.

Rare jaguars are hunted for their beautiful skins.

Polluted water is a threat to many species. Spilled chemicals kill birds and poison the food that many species depend on.

Sharing the world

Species all depend upon each other. If one species disappears altogether, others in turn become endangered. People, just like other animals, must share the world and its resources. A healthy planet needs all species to live together in a natural balance. Special organizations, international laws, and nature reserves can all help to protect endangered species and the places where they live, called habitats. Scientific research also helps us to understand more about life on Earth so that we can look after it better. Most importantly, people must learn to live in a way that does not damage the planet for all the species that live on it—including ourselves.

Species and Extinction

Going, going, gone

Over time, life adapts to changes in Earth's climate and environment. Some species gradually die out and new ones take their place. When a species dies out it is said to have become extinct, which means it has gone forever. Endangered species are species that are approaching extinction.

The greatest biodiversity is found in tropical rainforests.

◀ Species together

A species is a single, unique type of plant or animal, such as a jaguar. Nobody knows exactly how many millions of species exist, but we do know that all species depend on each other. The total variety of species in any place is called biodiversity. Biodiversity keeps our environment healthy and gives us a beautiful world to live in. To protect endangered species, biodiversity must be maintained.

Dead as a dodo

Many species that once shared our planet have already gone. When sailors first landed on the Indian Ocean island of Mauritius in the 1500s, they discovered the dodo. By 1693, this large, flightless bird had become extinct.

▼ Ancient extinctions

Dinosaurs became extinct sixty-five million years ago. It is thought they died out when a giant meteorite struck Earth, causing huge changes to the climate and environment.

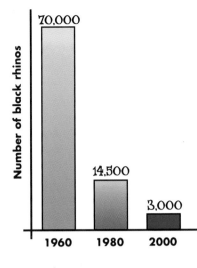

Number of black rhinos

70,000

14,500

3,000

1960 1980 2000

◀ Rare rhinoceros

Just one hundred years ago, black rhinos were common in Africa. They were hunted in great numbers, and in the last forty years their numbers have dropped sharply. Now they are one of the world's rarest large mammals, with fewer than three thousand remaining.

On the edge ▲

Some species may never technically become extinct because they can be preserved in captivity. But their numbers are so low that they have no future in the wild. Although there are a few captive Spix's macaws, there is now thought to be only one left in the wild.

▶ Too many people

People are responsible for the greatest wave of extinctions since the end of the dinosaurs. In the last two hundred years, as the human population has risen from one billion to six billion, more and more species have died out. Scientists think that up to thirty thousand species of plants and animals become extinct every year. At this rate, up to a third of the world's species may be lost in the next twenty years.

TALKING POINT

Q: If a meteorite strike had not killed off the dinosaurs, would they still be alive today?

A: We don't know. But birds are thought to be descended directly from dinosaurs, and today's crocodiles and tortoises are descended from animals that lived at the same time. People are now the biggest danger to all these animals.

CHAPTER TWO Hunting and Trade

Trigger happy

People have always hunted animals, but in the last few hundred years, advanced technology has made hunting more destructive. There are few places left for animals to escape the guns, nets, and traps of the hunter, and many species are being hunted toward extinction.

Wild food ▶

Early humans survived by hunting animals and gathering wild plants. Today, farming provides most of the food we need. But wild animals are still eaten in some places. In Central Africa, animals are hunted for this "bushmeat," and many species, including chimpanzees, are now highly endangered.

▲ Bad sport

Hunting for sport has driven many species to extinction. This includes the bluebuck in South Africa and the passenger pigeon in North America. Today, over five hundred million birds a year are shot in Europe as they migrate to and from Africa over the Mediterranean Sea. Many of these, such as the Eleonora's falcon, are endangered species.

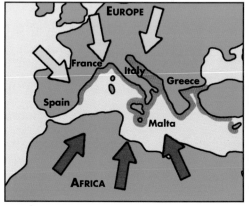

⬜➡ Autumn migration

⬛➡ Spring migration

🔴 Area where most birds are shot

◀ Trophy targets

Big game hunters prefer to kill the most impressive animals. Male lions are popular targets because of their magnificent manes. When adult male lions are shot, family life is severely disrupted. With no males to defend the territory of the pride, young lions have little chance of growing up.

Extermination ▶

People have never liked "problem" animals that compete with us for the same land or resources. Many endangered predators (animals that hunt other animals for food) are hunted because they threaten livestock. Wolverines in Norway are still hunted by sheep farmers. There are now thought to be fewer than 150 in the whole country.

◀ Poison trap

Poison or traps put out for predators often kill other creatures, too. In South Africa, sheep farmers put out poisoned bait to kill jackals that threaten their lambs. This poison also kills rare vultures that come to feed.

▶ Nets of death

Most modern fishing uses huge nets to catch thousands of fish at once. Many fish species are becoming rare due to overfishing. The Pacific bluefin tuna, a luxury food in Japan, has declined by ninety percent since 1960. Other creatures are also caught accidentally. Each year, thousands of harbor porpoises die in nets in the North Sea.

TALKING POINT

In the first national parks, predators like wolves or lions were shot to increase numbers of deer or antelope.

Q: Why shouldn't wolves and lions be shot? Wouldn't the world be a safer place without such killers?

A: With no predators to control numbers, deer and antelope overgrazed park land and soon there was not enough food. Many animals died. Scientists now know that predators keep populations of prey animals healthy by weeding out the old and the sick.

Making money

Many animals are killed for products made from their bodies. As the animals become rarer, the value of these products goes up and demand increases. Today, the international trade in wildlife products is worth over $20 billion per year.

▶ Whale oil

Whales were once heavily hunted for their oil, and some species almost died out. The northern right whale, once common, now numbers only a few hundred. Today, whale oil can be replaced by other products and most species of whales are internationally protected.

Tiger paw

▲ Tiger medicine

In some countries, especially China, rare animals are highly valued in traditional medicine. Tiger bones are believed to have special powers. It is hard to protect tigers from poachers—three subspecies are already extinct and there are now only about five thousand of these magnificent cats left in the wild.

▼ White gold

For hundreds of years, elephants have been slaughtered for their ivory, known as white gold, to make ornaments. In the 1980s, the elephant population fell by fifty percent as ivory prices rose. Today, the ivory trade is illegal. But some countries still want to make money from ivory.

▶ For the chop

Although many commercial trees are grown on plantations, others are still taken from the wild. Threatened hardwood trees such as mahogany, ebony, and teak are cut down for their timber, which is used to make expensive furniture and musical instruments.

Mahogany chest

▼ Leather

Rare reptiles such as turtles, crocodiles, and snakes are killed for their skins. The patterned skin of large snakes, such as the reticulated python, is used for fashionable shoes, belts, and bags.

Snakeskin boots

Reticulated python

▲ Fur trade

Many mammals are also killed for their skins. Some are farmed commercially, but others, such as the snow leopard, are still trapped in the wild. Its beautiful fur is used to make luxury clothing. The snow leopard is now highly endangered.

TALKING POINT

Animals such as cows are farmed and slaughtered to make leather from their skins.

Q: If you wear leather shoes made from cow skin, why not a fur coat made from cheetah skin?

A: Some people believe that killing any animal for its skin is cruel and unnecessary. But the cow is not an endangered species. Cows are farmed sustainably for meat, leather, and milk. Cheetahs are endangered. There are fewer than ten thousand left. We do not need cheetah skin, and if we continue to hunt cheetahs, there will soon be none left.

11

Wanted alive

Rare animals and plants are also in demand when alive. Although zoos no longer take animals from the wild, many rare species are captured to be used as decorations or pets. This endangers the wild population and also damages its environment. A lot of animals die during capture or transport.

Collectors' items

Rare tropical invertebrates, such as birdwing butterflies, are captured for private collections. In Hawaii, twenty-two of the forty-one Oahu tree snail species are now extinct, and the remaining nineteen are critically endangered.

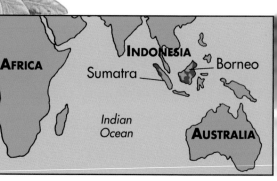

Oahu tree snail

■ Places where orangutans live

▲ Orphans

Rare primates, such as orangutans, are wanted for pets. Adults are killed to capture the babies. As these animals grow up and become harder to care for, their owners often get rid of them. Orangutans are found only on the islands of Borneo and Sumatra, where their forest home is fast disappearing.

◀ Pet reptiles

Rare and beautiful tortoises, snakes, and lizards are illegally smuggled around the world to be sold as pets. Transported under terrible conditions, many do not survive the journey. It is hard to care for wild reptiles in captivity. Many die.

Brown bear

► Dancing bear

Some animals are captured and held for amusement or sport. Rare Asian brown and black bears are used to entertain people by dancing, or by fighting dogs. The bears are kept chained up in cramped and cruel conditions.

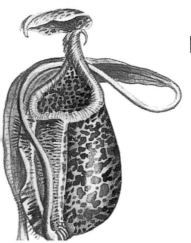

▲ Pretty as a pitcher

Many protected plant species are wanted alive. Pitcher plants are torn from their native soil in Borneo and sold to private collectors. The precious local environment is damaged in the search for these disappearing rarities.

► Falconry

In the sport of falconry, birds of prey such as peregrines are trained to hunt animals. Falconry is popular in the Middle East, and although some birds are bred for the sport, others are illegally taken from the wild. Eggs are stolen from nests and sold to raise birds in captivity.

▼ Going for a song

Millions of birds are trapped every year to be sold as caged songbirds. Many die. Macaws and other parrots have been very badly hit by this trade, and ninety different species now face extinction.

TALKING POINT

Q: What's wrong with keeping animals as pets if they're well treated and properly looked after?

A: There's nothing wrong with keeping a pet, such as a dog or a cat, if you know that it has been captive-bred. But with some animals it is very difficult to find this out for sure. Some animals are easy—and legal—to breed in captivity. Others are not, which is why they are taken from the wild.

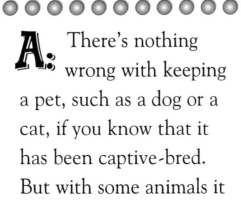

CHAPTER THREE

Disappearing Habitats

Endangered spaces

Earth's natural environment is being harmed by people. This is changing the face of the planet. Habitat destruction affects many species and is the biggest threat to biodiversity. To protect endangered species, we must protect the endangered spaces in which they live.

SOUTH AMERICA

About ninety percent of Brazil's Atlantic coastal rainforest has now been destroyed.

▲ Deforestation

Every year, over twenty-five million acres of forest are lost. Commercial logging destroys huge areas of forest in countries like Brazil. Forests are also cleared or burned by people who need land on which to live. As more people move into these areas, more trees are cut down for firewood or building materials.

▲ Homeless

Tropical rainforests probably contain between sixty and eighty percent of the land species on Earth, and they are disappearing fast. The golden lion tamarin of Brazil's Atlantic coastal rainforest is threatened by the loss of its habitat. Today, there are only about seven hundred of these tiny primates left.

◄ Kill or cure?

Rare western yews on the Pacific coast are being cleared to make way for logging. This useful and important tree contains taxol, a substance used to treat cancer.

◀ Green deserts

For wildlife, modern farms can seem like deserts. Crops are sprayed with chemicals, marshes are drained, and hedgerows are cleared to create bigger, more productive fields. A field that grows just a single crop does not support enough other plant and insect life for wildlife to survive. In Britain, butterflies and birds once common on farms are fast disappearing. The corncrake (left) is now endangered.

▼ Mangroves

Mangroves are tidal forests that line the seashore of many tropical countries. They provide food and shelter for unique wildlife, and their waters are important breeding grounds for reef fish. Mangrove forests around the world are being destroyed to make way for shrimp farms.

Hamilton's frog

Mangrove tree

▲ Overgrazing

Livestock can damage the environment for wildlife by destroying the ground vegetation and disturbing the soil. In New Zealand, Hamilton's frog has become very rare due to overgrazing by cattle and sheep.

TALKING·POINT

Q: With more people in the world, won't we need more land on which to grow food, even if this destroys habitats?

A: Not necessarily. Many poor countries have big debts. To pay these off, they grow crops, like coffee or tobacco, to sell to richer countries, rather than using the land to grow food for themselves. If poor countries could use more of their land to support their own needs, fewer habitats would be ruined.

Digging and building

Development and construction have damaged many habitats. The building of factories and roads, the expansion of towns and cities, and the mining of minerals all make a big impact on the natural environment. Many species are left homeless or are driven away.

▶ Turtle alert

Turtles need quiet, undisturbed beaches for breeding. But these beaches are threatened by the tourist industry. Beach sand is mined to use for building construction, and on some coasts, hotels and marinas have been built on important turtle nesting beaches. The bright lights disturb the turtles when they come ashore to lay their eggs at night. The green turtle is now an endangered species.

◀ Oil pipelines

Oil exploration in the Arctic affects many creatures that live there. New roads and mines damage the habitat of grizzly bears and millions of birds, such as snow geese. Oil pipelines that stretch across the land block the path of thousands of caribou as they migrate between their summer and winter feeding grounds.

Caribou migrate
in huge herds.

▶ Protecting penguins

Large, untouched reserves of valuable minerals lie beneath the frozen Antarctic. Many countries would like to exploit these minerals. However, there is now an international ban on mining in the Antarctic to protect the penguins and other wildlife that live there.

Roads ▼

Roads can spoil wild, undisturbed areas, and many animals are killed by road traffic. Many kangaroos in Australia die in this way. In Europe, barn owls are often hit by cars as they hunt for rodents on road shoulders at night.

Dams ▲

When rivers are dammed to produce hydroelectric power, habitats are flooded and destroyed. During the building of the Kariba Dam on the Zambezi River in Africa, many animals were drowned or displaced.

▲ Endangered salmon

The Atlantic salmon is becoming endangered. It is thought that dams built across rivers in Europe and North America may be preventing them from migrating upstream to breed.

TALKING POINT

Long fences have been built across the Kalahari Desert in Botswana to separate cows from wild animals.

Q: Isn't this a good thing? Fences help to protect wild animals.

A: Some animals need a lot of space. Wildebeest and zebra migrate across the Kalahari to find food and water. The fences block their path and many have died.

Making a mess

Huge amounts of waste are produced by people, from our factories, mines, cities, houses, and cars. Much of this waste ends up in the natural environment and causes great harm to wildlife.

Sea otters (left) are harmed by oil spilled from tankers (below).

▲ Poisoning rivers

When poisonous waste enters a river, the poison is carried downstream and can kill everything in its path. In January 2000, poisonous cyanide leaked from a gold mine in Romania into the Tisza River in Hungary. Over eighty percent of the fish were killed within hours, and some endangered species were completely wiped out. The river may never recover.

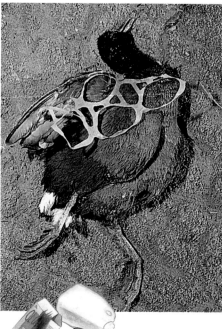

▶ Poisoning the sea

Oil spilled in the sea kills millions of marine creatures. In 1989, the oil tanker *Exxon Valdez* hit rocks off the coast of Alaska, spilling nearly eleven million gallons of crude oil. Up to three hundred thousand seabirds died. Other casualties included killer whales, common seals, and about five thousand rare sea otters.

Oil

▲ Plastic prisoners

Trash from our homes and towns, such as plastic drink containers, can be very dangerous to wildlife. Animals feeding on garbage dumps or on the seashore can be trapped, choked, or entangled in this waste.

► Egg damage

Chemicals sprayed on crops enter the food chain. The crops are eaten by small animals which, in turn, are eaten by birds of prey such as bald eagles. At each link in the chain, the chemicals become more concentrated. In the 1960s, the crop spray DDT weakened bald eagles' eggs so that they could not breed successfully. The population of these birds dropped until the chemicals were controlled.

TALKING POINT

Fossil fuels such as oil are to blame for much of the pollution that affects wildlife. Extracting fossil fuels damages habitats, burning them pollutes the air, and spillages can kill animals.

Q: If we don't burn fossil fuels, how will we get the energy we need?

◄ Up in smoke

In the late 1990s, huge areas of Indonesian rainforest were burned in some of the worst forest fires ever. Many of the fires, which destroyed the habitat of endangered species such as the orangutan, were started by people. Smoke filled the air for months, blotting out the sun.

A: Other energy sources that do not use fossil fuels—such as wind and solar power—are less harmful to the environment. We can do more to develop these alternatives.

► Troubled times

Animals are sometimes caught up in human problems. In 1994, a terrible war in Rwanda affected millions of people. It also affected the rare mountain gorillas that live in the country. Some were killed by soldiers, or by desperate people hunting for food.

Interfering with nature

Each habitat on Earth supports species suited to its particular climate and conditions. These species fit together in a careful natural balance to keep life in their habitat healthy. But people have seriously disturbed this balance. We have moved species into habitats where they don't belong. We have damaged habitats by changing the landscape and we have even altered the climate.

▼ Alien invaders

People have spread many animal and plant species around the world for farming or as pets. In their new habitats, these invaders can cause terrible damage to native species. When the predatory Nile perch was introduced to Lake Victoria in East Africa, it soon took over the lake, wiping out over fifty native species of fish within ten years.

Island species

Island species are easily threatened by alien invaders. The kakapo is a flightless parrot found in New Zealand that is adapted to life without predators. When people first brought dogs, cats, and rats to New Zealand, these invaders found the kakapos and their eggs to be easy prey. There are now only about fifty kakapos left in the wild.

In the last five hundred years, most mammal species that have become extinct have been on islands.

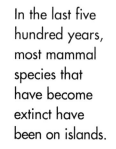

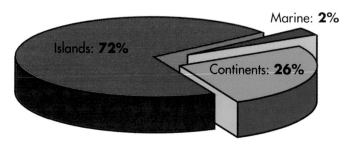

Islands: **72%**

Continents: **26%**

Marine: **2%**

► Disease

Domestic animals sometimes introduce new diseases to wild animal populations. If wild animals have never encountered these diseases before, they have no defense against them. In 1994, over a thousand lions in the Serengeti in Tanzania died from canine distemper introduced by dogs.

Warming up

Gases from pollution and forest fires—both caused by humans—enter Earth's atmosphere and trap the heat from the sun. This causes global warming, which affects our wildlife in many ways. Coral reefs around the world may be dying due to changes in sea temperatures. Coral reefs support a great diversity of marine species.

▲ Deadly seas

Warmer seas also cause growth of toxic algae on the sea surface. This poisons the marine food chain and threatens many sea creatures. The death of hundreds of endangered New Zealand sea lions in 1998 is thought to have been due to these algae.

▼ Melting ice

As the seas get warmer, the area of floating pack ice in the Arctic is decreasing. This causes problems for polar bears, which depend upon pack ice to travel between one hunting ground and another.

TALKING POINT

Domestic cats are alien invaders. They kill hundreds of millions of birds every year in the United States.

Q: What's the problem? Aren't cats part of the natural food chain?

A: No. They are fed and looked after by people, so there are far too many of them. Cats have a more serious effect on bird populations than any wild predator.

CHAPTER FOUR What to Do?

Safety first

It is not yet too late to save endangered species. Today, nature reserves and international agreements help to safeguard wildlife, and many organizations work to make sure this happens. Endangered species can be moved to safer areas and damaged habitats can be cleaned up and repaired.

▶ Safety for animals

The Ranthambore Tiger Reserve in India was created to give tigers a safe haven. Rangers patrol the reserve to keep an eye on the tigers and to protect them from illegal poaching. Money from visitors is used for the conservation of tigers.

▲ Safety for habitats

The Okavango Delta in Botswana covers over 5,800 square miles. This huge wetland is a vital refuge for wildlife. An international agreement called the Ramsar Convention protects important wetlands around the world.

Getting organized

Organizations protect endangered species in different ways. The World Wide Fund for Nature (WWF) has launched over eleven thousand conservation projects in 149 different countries.

A system of laws called the Convention on International Trade in Endangered Species (CITES) bans trade in endangered species (called Appendix 1 species) and controls trade in those that might become threatened (called Appendix 2 species). Environmental groups like Greenpeace (right) take direct action to obstruct activities such as whaling. Their bravery publicizes the plight of endangered species.

▼ Captive breeding

Some endangered species have been saved by captive breeding. In 1972, the last few wild Arabian oryx were rescued and transported to zoos in the United States. Here they bred successfully, and after ten years a small population was reintroduced to the wild. Now there are over three hundred wild oryx protected in Oman.

▲ On the move

Sometimes rare animals can be returned safely to their former home. In 1993, wolves were successfully reintroduced to Yellowstone National Park, where seventy years before they had been exterminated by hunters. Now their numbers are on the rise again.

▼ Cleaning up

In the 1970s, the number of otters in Britain fell drastically because of the heavy pollution of rivers. Now that the health of many rivers is improving—due to controls on industrial pollution—otters are beginning to return to their old haunts.

TALKING POINT

There are now only about 160 California condors left. Lots of money is spent each year trying to prevent their extinction. This money could preserve large areas of tropical rainforest and protect many other threatened species instead.

Q: Is it right to spend so much money on just a few birds, when it could be used better elsewhere?

A: Conservation is a difficult balancing act. The top priority for scientists is to protect biodiversity, but it is hard to let a well-known creature disappear without trying to save it.

Finding out more

We need more research and information in order to understand endangered species so that we can protect them. There are many things we still don't know, but scientists are learning more all the time.

▶ Collaring the dog

Many rare carnivores, such as African wild dogs, travel very long distances in search of food. In some areas, scientists have fitted collars containing tiny radio transmitters onto a few dogs. Special satellite equipment picks up signals from the collars, allowing scientists to track the movements of the dogs. This has taught us much about wild dogs—where they go and why—which helps us to protect them.

▼ Invisible voices

By studying and recording their behavior, scientists have discovered that whales have a complicated language. Whales use infrasound—low-frequency noises that travel great distances underwater. Infrasound enables whales to communicate and to find their way when migrating across the oceans.

▶ Cause and effect

Scientists need to study the whole
environment in order to understand
problems affecting certain species. Recent
research suggests that the overfishing of
sand eels in the North Sea could be very
harmful to seabirds. Many, such as puffins,
depend on these tiny
fish for their food.

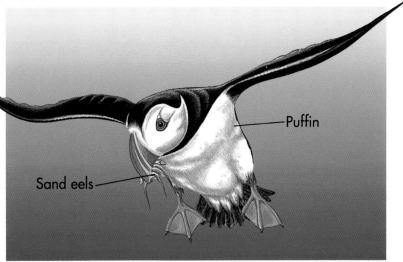

Puffin

Sand eels

◀ Living fossil

Scientists once thought that the coelacanth had died out
along with the dinosaurs. But in 1938, they first saw one
of these ancient fish, caught by fishermen in the Indian
Ocean. More coelacanths have since been discovered off
the coasts of Madagascar and Indonesia. Nobody knows what other
mysterious fish may still lurk in the ocean depths.

▶ New discoveries

In 1992, scientists were amazed
to find a new animal in the
forests of Vietnam. Called the
saola, it looks like a cross
between an antelope and an ox,
and has no known relatives.
Since this discovery, several more
new mammal species have been
found in the same region.

TALKING POINT

Q: Isn't it cruel to make a wild dog wear a radio collar? Shouldn't wild animals be allowed to live without interference?

A: Sadly, there are few safe places left for wild dogs. If we do not intervene, they will soon be gone. Knowledge gained from studying wild animals will help us to protect many more in the future. Scientists make sure that collars do not hurt or inconvenience wild animals.

Working together

Many endangered species are found in poor, developing countries. Here, people may hunt rare animals to get money to feed their families, or cut down protected forests for land to grow food. Poor countries need help to meet their basic needs so they can look after their own natural environment.

◀ Sustainable use

Sustainable use means taking resources from nature without damaging the environment. For years, rubber tappers in Brazil have collected latex from trees without destroying the forest. Local communities harvest sustainable yields of rubber and other nonwood products from the forest. The people get what they need without ruining the forest.

▶ Sharing space

There is still room for endangered species and people to live together. Biosphere reserves protect important rainforests that are home to many rarities. Here, local people live on the edge of the forest in areas called buffer zones, where they use the land sustainably. The community works together to manage the park and preserve its resources.

Sustainable farming in buffer zones

◀ Education

People in developing countries who work on the land often don't have the chance to go to school. Today, countries such as South Africa are building for the future by teaching all children about conservation. Young people who learn about the environment today can help to protect it tomorrow.

Replanting

About eighty percent of the plant species on the island of Madagascar are found nowhere else on Earth. Plants provide food, fuel, shelter, and medicine, but as Madagascar's forests are cleared, many species are disappearing. Today, in Madagascar's Plant Conservation Program, people study local plants and learn how to harvest, protect, and replant the right species.

▼ Ecotourism

Today, many people want to see endangered species for themselves, shooting them with a camera rather than a gun. Taking vacation trips to see wildlife is known as ecotourism. By spending money in the country they visit, ecotourists encourage that country to protect its wildlife. Visitors to Kenya's Masai Mara Reserve can see endangered species, such as cheetahs, or even enjoy the view from a balloon.

Although trade in ivory is currently banned, in some African countries hunters can pay to shoot elephants for sport. The money goes to the local community to meet the people's needs and to protect the environment.

Q: How can elephants be protected by hunting them?

A: It is a difficult question. Some people think it is wrong. Many local people argue that the hunters' money gives them a good reason to protect their land and the wildlife. What do you think?

Look Back and Find

How much do you know about endangered species? You can look back through the book to find answers to the questions on these pages. There are also some additonal facts to increase your knowledge and make you think.

Extinction

When did the dodo become extinct? Can you name another bird in danger of extinction today? Have people always been responsible for extinctions?

Extinction is part of nature. Many animals, including dinosaurs, became extinct long before there were any people on Earth. But today, we are causing the extinction of more species than at any time since the dinosaurs.

Hunting the hunters

Where are wolverines found? Why are they so endangered?

Wolves, cheetahs, brown bears, and golden eagles are among many other rare hunters that are themselves hunted by people in different parts of the world. Today, farmers in Europe and the United States get compensation for domestic animals that they lose to wild predators.

Murder for medicine

In what way are tigers threatened by traditional medicine? Where in the world is this medicine used?

Other species in danger from the traditional medicine trade include bears, killed for their gall bladders, and rhinos, killed for their horns, which are ground up into a medicinal powder. These products are not needed for treating sick people. They can easily be replaced by other medicines.

Great apes

Where are wild orangutans found? Can you name two of the threats that they face?

All ape species are endangered. In central Africa, chimpanzees and gorillas face threats similar to those faced by orangutans and gibbons in Asia—their forest homes are being destroyed, and the animals themselves are hunted for food and to supply the pet trade.

Deforestation

What are the main reasons for deforestation?

In recent years, much of the worst deforestation has been in tropical forests in poor, developing countries. But the past has seen extensive deforestation in Europe, the United States, and the rest of the developed world. Britain was once covered in thick forest, which was cleared for farming hundreds of years ago.

Mining

Mining poses a threat to many habitats. Can you name two different products that are mined? Name one place that is now safe from mining.

In addition to the mines themselves, new access roads encourage further unwelcome development. Chemical waste may pollute the land. Once the minerals are exhausted, the roads, dumps, quarries, and pollution scar the landscape for many years to come.

Oil spills

How many sea creatures can you name that are affected by oil pollution? Can you name where and when an oil disaster took place?

Seabirds such as guillemots spend nearly all their lives at sea. They fish from the surface, so they are very vulnerable to oil pollution. Oil damages their feathers and destroys the natural waterproof coating. When preening, the birds transfer the oil to their mouths, where it poisons them.

Alien invaders

Why did fifty species of fish disappear from Lake Victoria in a decade? Where do alien species often cause the greatest damage?

Alien plants can also cause serious problems. Eucalyptus trees introduced from Australia have flourished in southern Africa. But here they have contributed to drought by consuming far more groundwater than the native species require.

Captive breeding

Where were Arabian oryx bred in captivity? Where were they reintroduced to the wild?

Other successful reintroduction programs around the world include golden lion tamarins in Brazil, white rhinos in South Africa, and white-tailed sea eagles in Scotland. Reintroduction can only be done after careful study to make sure the natural habitat is suitable.

New discoveries

What is infrasound? What have scientists discovered about the language of whales?

Elephants also use infrasound. By making low, rumbling noises, they can communicate with each other over many miles. These sounds are often too low for humans to hear. Infrasound enables elephants to express warning or distress, or just to keep in touch with each other.

Ecotourism

What is ecotourism? How can it help protect endangered species? Name a popular destination for ecotourists.

Ecotourism can sometimes create environmental problems. In some places, such as the Galapagos Islands in the Pacific, the high number of visitors has damaged the fragile environment. Today, visitor numbers are carefully controlled.

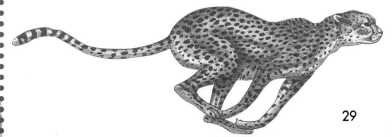

You Be Environmental!

You might think that many endangered species, like tigers, turtles, or parrots, live too far away for you to help them. But wherever we live, we all share the same air and the same oceans, so we are all connected to the same endangered spaces. You can help protect the environment by using water and energy more carefully. Walk or ride a bike instead of taking a car, recycle household waste, and don't leave litter. Together, all these small things will make a big difference to our disappearing wildlife.

Think before you buy

When you are on vacation, don't buy anything made from wild animals, such as seashells, coral, ivory, or snakeskin. If demand for these products decreases, then the animals and their habitats will be safer.

Useful addresses

Wildlife Conservation International
The New York Zoological Society
Bronx Zoo, New York 10460

Friends of the Earth
1025 Vermont Avenue NW, Washington, DC 20005. Website: www.foe.org

Greenpeace
1436 U Street NW, Washington, DC 20009
Website: www.greenpeaceusa.org

Your own nature reserve

Wherever you live, wildlife needs your help. Even common garden creatures such as thrushes, sparrows, and frogs are becoming rarer. Create a mini nature reserve by leaving a wild corner in your backyard, where wild plants will provide food and habitat for birds, insects, and other animals.

GLOSSARY

Biodiversity
The total variety of species of animals and plants, either in the world or in any one habitat.

Bushmeat
The name given to wild animals killed for food, particularly in central Africa.

Convention
A formal agreement made between countries or organizations to make sure that they all follow the same rules.

Extinction
The dying out of an animal or plant species. A species is said to have become extinct when there is no longer a living representative of it on Earth.

Food chain
A series of animals and plants that each depends upon the next for food. If one animal disappears, the whole chain may break down.

Fossil fuels
Fuels such as coal, oil, and gas formed in the past from the remains of living things. When they burn, they give off gases that pollute the atmosphere.

Habitat
The natural home of any living thing.

Invertebrates
Animals without backbones, such as insects, spiders, snails, and crabs. Mammals, birds, reptiles, amphibians, and fish have backbones and are called vertebrates.

Migration
The seasonal journey of animals from one place to another. For example, swallows that breed in Europe in summer fly in winter to Africa, where it is warmer and insect food supply is more plentiful.

Predator
An animal that hunts and eats other animals for food, such as a tiger, a hawk, or a shark.

Primate
A member of the monkey or ape family, such as a tamarin, a baboon, or a gorilla.

Reintroduction
Returning a wild animal to its natural habitat—a place where it once lived before it was exterminated by people.

Species
A single, unique kind of living thing. Normally only members of the same species are able to breed together and produce healthy offspring. Subspecies are different forms of the same species found in different regions.

Sustainable
Able to keep going continuously without being used up or worn out. Sustainable use of natural resources means taking what we need from the environment without damaging it for the future.

Wetland
A habitat that is mostly underwater, such as a swamp, marsh, estuary, or mangrove forest.

INDEX

Picture Credits

Abbreviations: t-top, m-middle, b-bottom, r-right, l-left, c-center.

Cover & pages 4, 5, 7 both, 15tm & m, 17b, 18 both, 21, 22-23c, 26m & b & 27b - Bruce Coleman Collection. 8, 13t, 14b, 16 & 26t - Eye Ubiquitous. 10m, 11, 17t - Oxford Scientific Films. 10b, 12, 14m, 19m, 20, 24l & 27t - Frank Spooner Pictures. 24r - Mike Unwin. 13m, 15tl, 19t - Stockbyte. 23tr - Digital Stock.